GUNNER

POEMS

by

GERRY MCFARLAND

Wandering Aengus Press
Eastsound, WA

Copyright © 2021 Gerry McFarland

All rights reserved

This book may not be reproduced or transmitted in any form by any means, electronic or mechanical, including photocopying and recording, or by any information storage and retrieval system. Excerpts may not be reproduced, except when expressly permitted in writing by the author. Requests for permission should be addressed to the author at gmcfarland@earthlink.net.

First Edition published by Wandering Aengus Press

Poetry
ISBN: 978-0-578-85742-8
Printed in the United States of America.
Author Photo: Allegra McFarland
Cover Design: Jill McCabe Johnson

Wandering Aengus Press
PO Box 334 Eastsound, WA 98245
wanderingaenguspress.com

Wandering Aengus Press is dedicated to publishing works to enrich lives and make the world a better place.

for Bob

The names of the sailors killed while serving in the Gulf of Tonkin, aboard the USS King, when it caught fire on May 23rd, 1969 are listed below:

                                    Milton Brown, BT3
                                    Joseph Fischer, BT3
                                      Kenneth Grubb, BT2
                                    Eugene Ware, BT2

Table of Contents

Monsoon *1*

Gunner Covers Up *3*

Gunner and Chuck Ride *4*

Gunner Falls in Love *6*

Gunner Apologizes for Not Shooting *7*

Gunner Sweats the Small Stuff *8*

Gunner Tells What Happened *9*

Gunner Thinks About It *10*

Gunner Tries to Die *11*

Gunner Declines to Participate in The Revolution *12*

Gunner Opens Fire *13*

Gunner Experiences Cleansing of the Soul *14*

Gunner's Go-Go Girl Dream *15*

Gunner Gets His Sea Legs *18*

Gunner Sees for the First Time *19*

Gunner Drinks Again *20*

Gunner Thinks About Everything at Once *21*

Gunner Remains *22*

Sailor Bob and the Queen of Angels *23*

Monsoon

for Joyce

I want to tell you about the monsoon,
The plank bridge from the gate
Of Subic Bay Naval Station to Olongapo,
The yellow river children dived into for coins,
How the monsoon made Olongapo a lake

And the men into dark silhouettes slow as divers
On the dirt town's nameless single road.
The monsoon drenched this white-clad sailor,
American dollars hidden in damp shoes.
Pink and blue fringed canopies of jeepnees

Lurched and splashed the puddled road
Past monkey meat on fire drum spits,
The fountain ringed by stone faces chipped
In every election's gunfire, baby ducks
Thrown to alligators for a peso.

In the monsoon's spontaneous embrace,
My uniform translucent in the warm flood,
With the brown bottle of San Miguel
I drank outside in the mud
I thought of you in that clean and sunny yard

Your face like a pale blossom.
The monsoon baptized Olongapo,
Granted extravagant forgiveness,
Made the road dark slop, tin rooftops rattle.
That was my last visit to Olongapo City,

Long before Mt. Pinotubo plumed
Over Mindanao, Luzon, and thick gray dust
Grew to wind-blown shapes of pickup trucks
On the abandoned base, and Olongapo
Strangled in soft, hot feathers.

I've forgotten what you look like.
Never saw the Philippines beyond Olongapo.
Never saw the rain tree forest,
The swing of light in another country.
Olongapo, Olongapo,

I keep saying your name.
Olongapo, once full of sticks and gunfire,
Deepened in a new volcanic skin,
Jeepnees axles wound with the tendrils of the koa,
I enter your dark street with a shovel and axe.

Gunner Covers Up

On the way to Alameda Air Station, Oakland,
California, I roll white paint on the angled fantail stripe,
Half an X on the helicopter pad to help pilots
Find the ship in the dark. Then the giant stacks

Erupt roiling clouds, fists of black matter
Congealed in the gut of the USS King that
Like an emperor at a table belches blackened crap
Into the wind. "Keep painting!" Chief barks.

So I keep at it, watch chunky smoke lay deep
Into damp white paint I just put down, collect
On the fresh-dipped roller heavy now with shiny goo
Then pull back over black and lumpy junk.

"Keep painting!" So I keep at it. I look back
On the mottled runny line, the endless clouds
Of muddied excrement that falls where I just painted.
I understand. Push the other way to cover it up.

I believe—"Keep painting!"—I must keep at it.
Though I no longer see the light and dark of things
In the rolling windy boil and smoke, I believe!
I understand; I have more paint than they have grit.

GUNNER AND CHUCK RIDE

After drinking all day, a drive-in movie
Was dullsville, man, so we blew the joint
In my Volkswagen, swigged from the Buds
In the open case. Chuck said:
Let's get the Harley, put the wind in our hair.
Far out, man, I said. Just the thing,
And I swung the bug down Strange Street
And stepped on it. Didn't see the thick,
White-painted posts at the end of the road,
Drove right between and swept
Like an albatross down the steep,
Wooded gut, blacked out, and stopped
At the trunk of a California oak.
When I came to, blood ran down
Chuck's sleeping face. I touched the handle
And the door thumped the dirt and I fell out,
Face up in the cool, soft soil and I dreamed
I was at sea, calm and slow in the dark
Under stars and the swells whispered
Like angels. I heard Chuck's voice.
Glass still breaking.
One front tire still wobbled catawampus.
The black windshield gasket dangled
from a branch like a giant rubber band.
Then Chuck stood over me like a bloody vision
Of mercy under heaven's dark trees,
His face blood red and his lips moving.
I crawled on hands and knees
Toward the white angels whispering
Hymns from the top of the hill
Until they grew silent and still,
But I could see them above me in white robes
Not singing, looking down at me
Crawling up toward them, but when I
Reached them they had turned to wood,
Flakes of white paint broken loose and falling.

I could still hear them, their many voices
Thick and heavy, louder and louder.
Lights flashed; my hands disappeared
And the angels, now wearing black
With guns on their hips, put their hands on my head
And blessed me into the open seat
Of the black and white car.
Chuck stood by a huge red truck. An angel
In white anointed his forehead. Lights
Filled the forest, brilliant and splashing.
My throat burned, my head throbbed,
My stomach felt hard and sharp and I thought
I was going to be sick but only words came out
Swollen and thick: It's alright, man,
I told them. You guys are doing your job.
I'm a drunk, and we're all brothers.
I sat all night on a concrete floor,
Gambled with cigarettes.
Released at dawn on my own recognizance,
An aimless boat, I floated
to the shore of the first open bar.

Gunner Falls in Love

Among the crew lined up
In whites standing and talking at parade
Rest on the foc'sle of the ship
Gunner saw the island of Honshu

Starboard, the green hills sculptured
Into steps, the green uncommonly
Green, bright and deep as the sun
On the swells. Asahi was sweet, the rice

Salty, the girls, smelling of powder
Spoke a tide of consonants.
Her breath warm and soft on his cheek.
So this was love in the dark. Like hiding.

Everything was closed. Everyone
Was gone but the girls in green silk
Leaning in doorways down the narrow
Alleys lighted with angled neon.

Gunner drifted, drunk, without
Order, foreign, unable to speak
His love in the strange dark town. They sang
To him like crickets: Buy me drink? Buy me drink?

Gunner Apologizes for Not Shooting

Somewhere over the hot water lay the enemy.
Don't know what they're gonna do, Captain says,
Our faces parallel at battle stations.
Sure, we're nuclear. But they're crazy.
Keep your butt up, boy.

The rivet of my helmet dug into my scalp.
Nothing anywhere but ocean.
The enemy is always invisible, Captain says.
Brace yourself like a tripod
Until it's time to shoot.

My flak jacket hung on me. The flacking
Started eight inches below my shoulder.
Plenty of room for a small rocket
Or a series of shells in a neat parabola
To find me and my bowl of a helmet.

The best defense is a good offense, Captain says.
Shoot first. Two facts, Captain says, in military life:
Follow any lawful order; and all orders are lawful.
Watch the endless horizon endlessly. Breathe,
Bend your knees, grip the gun as if you would fall
Without it, the knuckle loose at the trigger. Wait
For the enemy. Hold your position for twenty-five years.

Gunner Sweats the Small Stuff

The Secretary of the Navy flies into the Tonkin Gulf
By helicopter to inspect the USS King. I shine
The fifty-caliber machine gun, fool with the belt of casings

Until the shells curve sweetly from the breach to the box
And paint the bulkheads until the insulation shines.
The Secretary strolls the deck and passageways smiling.

He disembarks in the helicopter, his elbow like a swell
As he waves back at us, a bellyful of steel workings
And we desire nothing but a story with an end

When we gather, paint-spattered, on the mess decks for the movie:
Ride Beyond Vengeance, starring Chuck Connors. Absent
Five years without a word to his woman, he squares his jaw

When he finds she's married someone else. *What now?* He asks himself,
Hand flat on his six-gun. Hatches latched open, the Gulf
Like new paint to the horizon and the moon a bright

Running light on the dark bow of the sky. The projector stops.
Chuck's lantern jaw twists sideways as the film dissolves.
Lights die out. Fresh paint in the passageways, executed

Yesterday, bubbles, melts and stinks in the hot smoke
When the after-fire room erupts in flames and the mess decks
Flood in black and roiling clouds. We shout and beat it,

Drum the deck and rattle the ladders in our pounding run.
The USS King, dead in the water, groans like a man.
Burned mates stumble forward choking to their knees.

Gunner Tells What Happened

From below where the tanks
Of heat boiled he surfaced, charred
Boots first, drenched with his last
Sweat, cheeks and forehead blistered

In perfect circumferences, islands
Of pink skin strafed by fire.
Tied in a metal stretcher still dressed
He stares off as if in thought

About to ask the time or tell
How he smelled his death and let go.
Bearing their damp shipmate forward
They navigate this new continent

On the dark deck of the
Disabled ship adrift and blind
In the Gulf of Tonkin, running lights
The only stars. How awkwardly

They set the body down. Their hands
Failed them. They return for the next
Body, three more yet, failing
Silently as young men do.

Gunner Thinks About It

The wind stirs the hair of the dead,
Their faces covered with Navy blankets,
Boots stick up at the other end.

Today we walked straight by, did not
Cry out as wives and daughters might.
Now, at 0300, nothing

Anywhere but the open sea
Rising and falling like it's breathing
In a dark and sullen mood.

Six days with a starboard list
At five knots from the Gulf to the yards
At Subic Bay Naval Station,

Philippines. The machine gun glistens
In what light there is. No wind.
The great hulk slips through.

Not much happens at five knots.
Burning chaos.
The night's few stars.

Gunner Tries to Die

The sea rolls off the end of the world.
Somewhere under the same sky is Nam.
In the invisible jungle the Unknown
Buddy wades in the infected

Muck, twigs in his hat, face
Painted green and black, elbows
Cradling the AK-47 swing
At night over the thick water

And lily pads. Gunner believes
His own heart is shot, hangs
On a wire from his neck purple as rage,
Or a prize. He dies then on the fan tail,

Clutches his shirt for the Unknown Buddy
Grimacing and sinking in
The novel swamp without him.
The USS King steams out of the Tonkin Gulf.

Out of the smoky towers
And muddy caverns by an itinerary,
A tidy printed protocol
Clean as the admiral's shoes, orders

To abandon the Unknown Buddy,
Lost anyway, breathing slime
Into his lungs sinking and dying.
Gunner looks back from the rolling fantail,

Over the wake of the frigate –
Imperial, blind and speechless.

GUNNER DECLINES TO PARTICIPATE IN THE REVOLUTION

After the Tet Offensive. December 1968

Poker, drunk at Suzie Bar
The women scoop my chips.

I laugh. We ain't nothing, I say,
But the small fish on the face of God.

Don't get me wrong, I say. It matters.
The brass got tired of being fools.

That's all. No revolution here.
They sent us communication techs.

Guys with steel eyes, wires in their ears
Who cheat at poker in the Tonkin Gulf

Then disembark in the chopper.
Their steel cabin says:

Top Secret
No Entry

In red on the door. No big deal.
No revolution here. Back in San Diego

Some long hair shouted at me: *Baby killer!*
I laughed. Far out!

No big deal. No revolution here.

Gunner Opens Fire

I know practice is as close as I will ever get to killing.
The fifty-caliber machine gun, cocked on its tripod,
Hot and smoking jumps when I open fire
On the empty oil drum bobbing on the South China Sea.

Spit casings ping on the deck like teeth into a steel bowl.
The tumbling shells arc in shooting pools of humid air.
I want it to explode in the damp jungle, the black land
Where death lives, but I can't even see it.

Someone used the word "fighting" once
And it killed me. To call this fighting was to call dancing
Combat, guns made of silk, and death a pair of heels.
For the enemy I can't see, I open fire. For the exempt,

Philosophizing under palm trees, dinner tables full
Of earnest pleading, for prim Silvia, hands in her lap,
Who wants to negotiate without raising her voice.
The girls saving themselves for better priests.

For the dark face in the rubber trees, the sniper's plug,
The invisible enemy, for the killing I'd take part in
If I could, make them hug themselves in the mud,
Pray for love, mercy, faith, all of it when I open fire.

Gunner Experiences Cleansing of the Soul

Drunk, shirt tail a-wag, they stop me
At the gate for being disheveled
Put me up against the wall, release me
To the warm fat-dropped monsoon,

A waterfall enough to drown any fire,
Cleanse any filth, alter any heart.
When I am drunk it is my job
To forgive. I stumble on the road.

Monsoon a crash of silver on the street
My uniform translucent I trip
And pitch to my hands and knees, spill
To the pavement, alone on the base.

They should see me now, I think,
As I push myself back up to my feet.
I forgive them. I raise my hands and face,
Drink the rain and look straight back at the dark.

Gunner's Go-Go Girl Dream

She turns on the bar top,
Face lifted to strobe-lit heaven,
Eyes closed, the little hills

Of her ankles fluid as the surf,
The mounds of her hips twin
Atolls that narrow

To the peninsula of her bare
Waist under spare dim
Lights. She is a human

Island in a long dark world
Of spilled beer and glitter.
Her face, like a moon lit up,

Tropical as sand.
Does she, floating like a moon
Over the ocean, desire?

My heart is at sea, my rudder
Shifts port to starboard,
Rises and falls in my body.

The stars of her own island
Planet blink. She dances
On the bar, long

As a dock, a harbor break
In the darkness, and we,
Her supplicants like little gigs

At the toes of her pointed shoes
Bob in her wind. The door
To the bar opens onto

Broadway in San Diego.
Horns crash, engines throttle
And lights from headlamps beam.

Streetlights reveal the bouncer,
Bored, sober, slumped
On his stool, checking IDs

With a flashlight. I could leave,
Unmoor from this dock. But the beer
Is cold and all there is

On the street are the hawks
Selling gilt-edged Bibles.
Here the light softens

On her skin, her hips
Drift in the rhythmic tide,
And her long, dark, curled

Hair falls on the swells
Of her breasts and gleams
like stars on the surface

Of a black sea on a clear night.
She dances in front of me,
Looks down at me from the glory

Of her painted face,
Into my adoration,
And dawns into a smile

Meant for me alone.
And I dream my hands on the wheel
Of a red Stingray top down

And bound for Tijuana
Her fingers in my hair
Tires rolling like the ocean.

Gunner Gets His Sea Legs

I know to get my sea legs I remain
Upright starboard aft in the hard turn,
My back to the wind so it can't
Force my breath back down my throat.
As the USS King rolls and falls in the swells,
Screws gulp and churn the foam, slice
The heaving breast of a live thing
That hoists a thousand-ton displacement
And heals the waters
From the machine's mad wake
Easily as a forgiving god.
I know to just hang on
When the sea is in a mood.
I know to keep my mouth shut
When the wind picks up, the sun drowns,
And I lean into the curve of the earth.

Gunner Sees for the First Time

That's how it is
On watch at 0300
The machine gun glistens
With oil in what light there is.
No wind. The great hulk
Slips through
Night and water equally.

Gunner Drinks Again

In Japan Asahi beer comes in huge bottles.
We grin at the girl, tip her and our glasses.
We stumble into the rest of the night,
A dark and dizzy country, shout,
Laugh, rejoice at the next door
To fling itself open so we can one more time
Express our yen for the smiling Mama San's
Permission and the sweet night,
Pass out, drag back for reveille,
Get sick, swear off, start over.

GUNNER THINKS ABOUT EVERYTHING AT ONCE

I toss the trash in a sealed plastic bag
Over the fantail to slowly sink, disintegrate
In the salt, disburse the crumpled cargo
scraps strewn across the centuries;

The bodies of sailors sunk with ships, or dropped
Into the sea in funereal sacks, litter
At the bottom of the world; 1,000
Tons of steel, aluminum, plastic,

And glass, gray and grim, turns and rolls
And the wind shears the face of the sea, the bow
Rises, falls, and shears the ocean's arc
That falls back into the great body,

Swirls into itself again, unchanged
Undiminished. A good day on the open sea,
I look down or sideways to breathe, my work clothes
Stretch and flag against my body; I lean

Into the wind, one arm across my chest
To keep my soul from blowing out; we all
Know how in a mood the heaving ocean rips
The ladders from their welds like buttons

On our dungarees; we dog the hatches,
Mouth the ocean swells, the ragged seas,
Twisted stanchions, the spool of steel cable
Snapped from its bracket, unwound silver
Shining like a water snake in the Gulf.

Gunner Remains

No more sailing. No more ships.
I take my walks on land
that sways like a ship's deck,
my body rocking still
without the wall of wind at sea.

I'm not drunk anymore,
so it isn't beer, but to be who I was
no longer seems impossible
on this damp deck,
awash in the swell of rain.

The grass in the park turns to water,
Pine becomes salt.
Of course, I think about the four men,
dead since 1971. They have become trees.
Grassy silent hills. Everything

is about death. Sometimes I forget that.
But the idea—death—remains
whether I think of it or not,
remains in the soil, beyond wishing,
beyond consciousness,
embodied in the darkening afternoon
among the silent men.

Sailor Bob and the Queen of Angels

> "Do you think you'll be the guy
> To make the queen of the angels sigh?"
> *The Doors*

Bob was always falling in love.
He was a sonar man, searching

Among the whales when submarines
Eluded him. Once he fell in love

With a woman on a first date, proposed,
She accepted, then broke it off

The next day. He called her, wanted
Explanation, definition,

Something discernible, but she
Was like a submarine

That never surfaced, only submerged.
Bob weathered disappointment,

Shifted rudder, came to a new course.
Of the ports in Japan, Sasebo

Was a favorite with the crew
And Bar Suzie was the busiest.

Bar Suzie was a stand bar,
Where women entered and left

Through a back door, but never came out
From behind the bar. There was a woman

In Bar Suzy, Keiko, whose large
Dark eyes shone like searchlights

Framed by her thick black hair,
That glistened like a dark sea.

Bob fell for her, to which
I said: "She's a whore, Bob."

"I just enjoy being with her," he said.
"She's a whore," I told him again.

In Bar Suzy, Bob sat across from Keiko
Until the last night when the USS King

Was to depart from Sasebo.
We were in formation on the foc'sle,

Waiting for the boatswain's signal
When I noticed a lone, Japanese

Woman standing on the pier.
Bob and Keiko kept this up

For three years, three tours
Of the Far East, and there she was

That morning, standing on the pier,
One hand raised briefly. Still,

I had to ask: "Is that . . . "
Bob nodded.

ACKNOWLEDGMENTS

"Monsoon"
Talking River and *The Making*

"Gunner Apologizes for Not Shooting"
Pontoon and *Hawai'i Pacific Review*

"Gunner and Chuck Ride"
Contemporary Voices

"Gunner Thinks About Everything at Once"
War, Literature & the Arts

"Gunner Tells What Happened"
Carquinez Poetry Review

"Gunner Falls in Love" and "Gunner Tries to Die"
Controlled Burn

About the Author

Gerry McFarland worked in carpentry before joining the US Navy, where he served 1968-72. He was a gunner's mate on the USS King. His interests since have evolved into writing, psychology and education. He was associate editor at Floating Bridge Press 2010-2016 and taught at University of Phoenix and Edmonds Community College. He graduated from Antioch University Seattle with a master's in psychology and an MFA in creative writing from the Rainier Writer's Workshop. His full collection of poems, *The Making*, was published by Cave Moon Press in 2019. His work has appeared in *Bellowing Ark*, *Contemporary American Voices*, *Crab Creek Review*, *Crucible*, *Limestone*, *Meridian Anthology of Contemporary Poetry*, *Pacific Northwest Magazine*, *Switched-on Gutenberg*, *Zyzzyva*, the anthology *Detours: Poems of Travel by Land, Air, Sea, and Mind*, and many others.

www.ingramcontent.com/pod-product-compliance
Lightning Source LLC
Chambersburg PA
CBHW051413290426
44108CB00015B/2267